great containers

great
containers

making • decorating • planting

Clare Matthews

photography
Clive Nichols

hamlyn

For my parents, Ruth and Geoffrey Smee

First published in Great Britain in 2004 by Hamlyn,
a division of Octopus Publishing Group Limited,
2–4 Heron Quays, London E14 4JP

Copyright © Octopus Publishing Group Limited 2004
Photographs © Clive Nichols

Distributed in the United States and Canada by
Sterling Publishing Co., Inc.
387 Park Avenue South, New York, NY 10016-8810

A CIP record for this book is available from the
British Library.

ISBN 0 600 60947 2

The author and publishers have made every effort to ensure
that all instructions and ideas given in this book are accurate
and safe, but they cannot accept liability for any resulting
injury, damage or loss to either person or property whether
direct or consequential and howsoever arising. The author
and publishers will be grateful for any information that will
assist them in keeping future editions up to date.

Printed and bound in China

10 9 8 7 6 5 4 3 2 1

contents

introduction

When many garden projects take years to mature, and others require a considerable investment of time and money, containers offer a welcome, quick-and-easy solution to enlivening and decorating an outside space. Container gardening has much to recommend it – almost any plant can be grown in a container, and anything that will hold enough compost can be used to accommodate it, so there is plenty of scope to create something imaginative. Mature plants can be used to create an instant display, while the small scale of container projects makes them an ideal testing ground for new planting ideas and colour combinations.

There is a plethora of uses for planted pots: successful containers provide instant colour and interest where there is none, terraces and walls can be softened with lavish planting displays, well-planted pots can highlight another garden feature – a gateway or bench perhaps – or stand alone as a conspicuous focal point. Lines or groups of pots can be used to divide or change spaces and plants can thrive in the smallest of pots to create a garden where there is none on balconies, stairwells and windowledges. In short, planted containers are an invaluable tool in shaping and furnishing the garden.

For maximum effect, the colour and style of a container and its planting should be tailored to its surroundings and its purpose. Customizing or producing your own containers not only adds personality and zest to the garden, but allows the freedom to design the perfect pot for any situation. Whatever the style or mood of an outdoor space, a container can be planted to suit.

The character and style of a container comes from many elements – the colour, shape and scale of both plants and pot, and how these interact. A mass of purple crocus in an exquisite gold urn might look opulent, but plant the same crocus in a wicker basket and the mood is of pretty rusticity. The most stunning results in container gardening are achieved when pot and planting are treated as a whole, so the colour, shape and form of both work together to create a hardworking garden feature with an appeal and intensity far greater than the sum of its parts.

Choose mellow terracotta and olive oil tins planted with vibrant geraniums to conjure up the spirit of the Mediterranean; architectural plants in bold containers to create a contemporary look; or cram pretty flowers into baskets and buckets to complement cottage garden planting. The deft use of containers can even impose a style or personality on a space where there is none.

This book contains six collections of containers and planting schemes, conceived to create or complement a particular garden theme or style. The containers and planting are designed to work together. Each collection contains inspiring ideas for decorative containers and stunning combinations of plants to enliven all kinds of gardens.

colour

Colour has the power to stir the emotions – some colours can be associated with a particular mood or feeling, others are redolent of a specific style or place. The manipulation of colour can be a powerful tool in honing the ambience or personality of a garden. Hot colours are exciting, dynamic and daring, cool colours lend an air of sophistication; rich, heavy colours have a seductive wealth and opulence. Used intelligently, the orchestration of colour permeates all parts of the garden, planting, hardscaping, furniture and containers to create a coherent pleasing effect. And so it should be with containers – the power of colour carefully harnessed to achieve stunning results.

red

Powerful, dominant and vibrant, red always seems to steal the show.

1 Set against a bright lime-green backdrop of foliage and presented in striking red mosaic tubes, the otherwise rather unremarkable blooms of red petunias become powerful and unavoidable.

2 Deeper blood reds are less demanding; they are richer and have a more subtle impact which can be used to good effect in many different settings.

3 This autumn planting of *Gaultheria procumbens*, *Skimmia reevsiana*, cyclamen and *Cotoneaster frigidus* 'Cornubia' has an energy and fire that is slightly restrained by the plain terracotta pot that houses it.

The energy and vigour of red make it irresistible to the eye. Many people caution its use or declare it too obvious, but if you want a container with enough personality to stand centre stage – with passion, daring and natural prominence – then red is the colour. In the garden, surrounded by green, its complementary colour, red will always sing out wildly with lively enthusiasm.

4 Large clusters of shining red berries of *Skimmia japonica reevsiana* bring life and dynamism to what would otherwise be a rather drab composition, and make it something really special.

5 Surrounded by rich red planting of dahlias, petunias and achillea, this bold red and black jar makes a daring, almost dangerous, focal point in the garden. It is planted simply with black *Ophiopogon planiscapus* 'Nigrescens'.

6 The voluptuous red blooms of the tulip 'Rococo' have an almost velvety quality – few reds are quite so rich and luxuriant.

pink

Pink can be soft, gentle and romantic – or shocking, vivacious and demanding.

1 The hard, uncompromising pink of *Tulipa humilis* Violacea Group 'Black Base' must be positioned and used with care.

2 In the pink, this vibrant planting uses flamboyant pinks contained within crisp box hedging. A cooler pink bowl is home to blooms of a similar colour and acts as a subtle focal point that is in complete harmony with its surroundings.

3 Growing through the lime-green and yellow blades of *Acorus* 'Ogon', spectacular pink *Tulipa humilis* Violacea Group 'Black Base' is matched by an equally spectacular pink pot. The use of the lime-green acorus emphasizes the shocking pink display.

Pink is a pastel colour, created from a combination of white and red, and its brightness depends on the amount of white it contains. Pale pinks are relaxing, undemanding and safe. A scheme of pale pink is unlikely to offend but is also unlikely to have star quality. At the other end of the scale are the high-spirited flamboyant pinks, difficult and demanding, but ideal for creating a spectacle.

4 The frilly pink and white flowers of *Cyclamen* 'Miracle' in their tiny painted jars make a charming, uncontroversial display suitable for many situations.
5 Pink on pink – here the same colour has been repeated in each of the three bowls to build up a high-voltage block of rich colour. The plants have been chosen carefully to echo the strong pink of the dazzling pots.
6 An unremarkable deep green glazed pot shows off the bold pink of a mass of the sturdy hyacinth 'Pink Pearl'. A lighter pink hyacinth would look washed out in such a dark-coloured, glossy container.

blue

Cool, restrained and remote, the character of blue is much affected by the colours around it.

1 A fairly dramatic blue painted pot is softened and made pretty with a charmingly flowery summer combination of white cosmos, *Delphinium* 'Delfix' and *Nierembergia scoparia* 'Mont Blanc'.

2 Silver, white and lilac-blue work together to create a cool, composed display made pretty by the delicate blooms of the violas and stocks. This small group of plants will produce the most wonderful fragrance that can only heighten its appeal.

3 In well-weathered terracotta pots, blue *Muscari armeniacum* combine with the fulsome yellow tulip 'Mr Van Der Hoef' to give a cheerful spring show.

Alone, blue can be bland, unexceptional and recessive. It is a safe colour, lacking in emotion, but can be used in a variety of ways. With white, it is cool and icy, with yellow it is more exciting, but bouncing off orange the result is lively and dynamic. True blue flowers are a rarity; beware of so-called blue-flowered plants that would, in reality, be better described as mauve or purple.

4 The dainty flowers of *Delphinium* 'Delfix' are an arresting true blue, usually hard to find. This plant has great potential for combining with other bright colours for a really eye-opening effect.

5 The contrast between the blue pots and the lime-green backdrop enlivens what would otherwise be a very chilly scene.

6 Sparkling true blue glass mulch shows off the fleshy blue-green leaves of the succulent *Aeonium* 'Peacockii'. It is not just the plants which can be used to achieve the desired colours – pots and mulches offer great opportunities too.

orange

Warm, spicy and zesty, orange has a positive, sunny and sometimes dramatic personality.

1 Handsome orange pumpkins held in a glowing copper container make an unusual and appropriate addition to a grouping of containers for an autumn display. The pumpkins will last for many weeks.

2 Set against the black of a handsome metal container and the sword-shaped leaves of *Ophiopogon planiscapus* 'Nigrescens', even the flowers of the humble pansy have an intensity that is arresting.

3 Rich and coppery miniature chrysanthemums create a rather muted display, still warm but mellow, redolent of falling leaves and shortening days.

Coppery, deep oranges have a richness and autumnal associations, while the brighter, clear shades of orange are full of life and energy to add zest at any time of year. Oranges sparkle most when set off by clear blues, lime-greens and purples. Combine orange with shades of yellow, gold and red, however, and the result is cheerful sunny accord.

4 Wild and blazing, and definitely demanding to be noticed, this extravagantly painted orange container almost radiates heat – love it or hate it, it will certainly steal the show in just about any setting.

5 The paper-thin petals of *Papaver nudicaule* are a true clear orange. When lit by the sun, they become incandescent.

6 A solid block of orange, this contemporary container dominates the scene. It is made from sheets of shocking orange acrylic, and has a light inside which makes the top of the container glow in the dark.

yellow

Cheery and bright, yellow is the light-hearted colour of the sun, which gently draws the eye.

1 Sober and sophisticated, these mustard-yellow containers complement the green of the smartly clipped box bushes beautifully.

2 This joyful spring display has a harmony generated by the combination of yellows and lime-green. The colour of tulip 'Golden Girl', *Narcissus* 'Yellow Cheerfulness' and the pansies is actually emphasized by the lilac-blue backdrop.

3 A clear, strong yellow matched by a strong pink produces a spirited planting. A weaker yellow would look drained against this pink, while a weaker pink would look insipid next to this vibrant yellow – either way the container would lose its appeal.

Yellow is a versatile colour and one that abounds in the garden, from pale yellows with a fresh purity, through clear yellows, to deeper golden yellows. In containers, yellow can be used to create a number of effects – clear bright yellows are eye catching, paler yellows are suited to simple pretty displays, while the deeper golds and mustards reflect less light and have a more opulent feel.

4 Serenity and calm emanate from this pale yellow lily, quite a different personality from its wild and wayward orange and red relatives. Though essentially the same in form, colour prescribes the flower's personality.
5 Looking like it radiates the warmth of the sun, a mass of yellow violas is a straight-forward but stunning way to plant a pot.
6 Yellow used in dramatic contrast to black on this grand scale can have a truly theatrical effect. This painted urn is planted with the yellow stems of *Cornus stolonifera* 'Flaviramea' to make a stunning winter display.

white

Creating an effect of innocence, yet elegant and sophisticated, white is the colour of light.

1 Stately, yet not without glamour, this black and white combination with 'Mont Blanc' lilies makes a fragrant welcome for a smart entrance. A second identical container stands on the other side of the door to form a pair of sentries.

2 Brilliant white on white, the planting and the containers work together to bring about a dazzling contemporary effect. The look is enhanced by the complementary grey pebbles arranged around the pots.

3 Looking like patches of bright light, these white hyacinths lift an area of neutral hardscaping, leading the eye to the white viburnum in the background.

White blooms have the power to brighten dark corners and dazzle in full sun. White is composed, restrained and the perfect choice for containers where the mood is one of elegance and calm. It works well with greys and silvers and makes the perfect cool companion for blue. Put white blooms among dark green foliage or a dark backdrop and they will appear even whiter.

4 The austerity of black and white stripes is elegantly complemented by the dark foliage and flowers of *Skimmia japonica* 'Rubella'.

5 The robust flowers of *Rhododendron* 'Alpen Rose' create a strong block of white and will remain on the plant for several weeks in early summer. The flowers stand out particularly well against such dark foliage.

6 Black and white cannot fail to look good together. These quirky zebra pots are pure fun – a mulch of black crushed glass ensures the colour theme stays pure and is not diluted by the brown of compost.

silver & grey

The sleek, clean lines of metal containers are the essence of contemporary style.

1 The solidity of this polished stainless steel tub is perfectly balanced by the rigidity of *Agave americana*. The agave relishes a sunny spot and needs protection from frost.
2 Containers designed for indoor use may last a few seasons outdoors. This reflective metal waste paper bin gives a lift to the fleshy grey rosette of echeveria. A mulch of grey slate finishes the composition.
3 The sheer area of mirrored metal in this group grabs attention. Simply planted with elegant astelias and an agave, the striking appearance of these containers belies their humble origin in the laundry. This group is smart and impressive.

Combine the cool reflectivity of silver tubs with the strong forms of grey-leaved architectural plants to create a mood of sophistication. Plant the same silver container with dazzling white blooms such as lilies or tulips, and the effect is chic but softer. Or grow blue or pink flowers through the silver foliage of *Artemisia* 'Powis Castle' and the result is fresh and unsentimentally pretty.

4 The soft grey-green of its leaves and the exquisite form of this unusual agave make it a real star; the voluptuous curve of the container contrasts perfectly with the spiky form of the agave.

5 A host of fragrant white lilies in an aluminium container instantly softens the brashness of this polished group. The look is sleek but less harsh.

6 A single small container can lack presence and become insignificant – a group of three or five is eye catching. Repeating a simple composition creates a minimalist look and is a good way to make something out of not a great deal.

making containers work

The real skill in container gardening is not just in concocting amazing combinations of plants and containers, but in using them well in the right setting. Planted containers are a valuable tool – they allow the gardener to decorate the garden and change the way a space is perceived, to create drama and interest where there was none, and to highlight and enhance other garden features. Few gardens do not have spaces that would benefit from the addition of a well-chosen container; the aim is to create the right container for the right spot – the right colour, the right size, the right style, the right planting – so it is well suited to its location and its purpose.

changing space

A row of pots or planters is a simple and inexpensive option when it comes to dividing or changing outside spaces; it can direct the eye and determine how space is perceived.

This infinitely flexible solution is also blissfully temporary, allowing radical changes in a garden's layout with no lasting effect. You may want to develop a more intimate dining space on a large terrace by encircling it with pots, divide and screen areas of the garden that have different styles, or create privacy. It is amazing how effective a row of containers can be.

ABOVE Though small and rather unremarkable in themselves, these pots of ornamental kale make an effective boundary.

LEFT This large expanse of decking is divided into more intimate spaces by large wheeled planters that are easily moved to redefine the space.

grouping containers

Gathering a group of containers together to create a display has many advantages. Eye-catching displays are easily built up, pot by pot, to soften difficult corners, decorate terraces or to act as focal points.

Firstly, though each member of the group may not be special, or may even seem a little lack lustre, once carefully arranged together the resulting group can look impressive. Building up a collection of pots, rather than planting in one or two large containers, means the arrangement can be given good shape and balance, which can be adjusted as one member of the group goes over and another comes into its own.

The success of a group lies in choosing plants and containers that work well together. This gives the display a unity, while including a variety of textures and shapes for interest. Working around a colour theme can be a safe and reassuring way to start building a display.

LEFT Crowding spring bulbs into containers makes for a stunning display. Planting the same bulbs in pots of different heights means the colour can be built from the ground up. Small pots can be raised up on bricks to play a role at the back to get the composition just right.

ABOVE The temporary nature of containers means you can have fun and try out combinations – when you tire with it, the pots can be regrouped. Other props have been included in this autumn scene: pumpkins, a pot of hazelnuts, and a copper-coloured glass bauble.

sentries

Flanking a bench, gateway or some other garden feature with a pair of containers gives it emphasis and import. To perform such sentry duty, containers must have a strong presence and be scaled up to make an impact and be noticed.

ABOVE With their soft, romantic pink planting, these old stone urns work sympathetically with the stone of the steps on which they stand, gently drawing attention to their presence.

ABOVE RIGHT These lofty sentries of clipped holly mark the boundary of lawn and gravel.

RIGHT These theatrical sentries have atmospheric lighting.

windows, steps & tables

Small pots and troughs with dainty planting in scale with the container are all that is required to enliven windowledges, steps and tabletops. Often close to eye level, these spaces offer a great opportunity to perfect small-scale designs, with plenty of detail.

Intricately formed blooms and foliage, though small, can be shown off to their best advantage when viewed close up. Choose diminutive bulbs, little rock plants or culinary herbs to be appreciated at close quarters. Scent is an important quality too, in these areas where you regularly pass by.

LEFT An eclectic array of metal containers has been arranged with panache to dress these steps with culinary herbs.

BELOW Easily lost in a crowd, the seemingly frail blooms of *Iris reticulata* can be admired in this windowsill display.

ABOVE A planted trough or a row of three or five small pots will make a successful centrepiece for a rectangular table. Round tables are best adorned with a single central pot. Here, white hyacinths in wicker troughs make deliciously fragrant decorations.

focal points

Whether they are marked out by a statuesque form, bold colour, or by a contrast with their surroundings, focal points have to stand out from the crowd if they are to be effective.

Focal points should be engaging points of interest, the star performers of a particular garden scene or vista. This usually demands both size and personality of note, but as always, these characteristics should fit comfortably with the ambience of the garden around them.

ABOVE With elegantly arching, evergreen fronds, *Butia capitata*, set in a sympathetic blue-green container, makes a substantial focal point that is unchanged by the seasons.

LEFT The purple globes of the giant *Allium giganteum,* housed in a container of a similar hue, produce an unconventional focal point that seizes the attention.

ABOVE In this verdant knot garden, a clipped standard quietly adds height and interest at the end of each of the paths.

RIGHT Single, choice specimens often make stunning focal points; this beautiful Japanese maple is no exception.

making containers work **31**

opulence & riches

The rich, sumptuous colours of this collection bring a sense of luxury and indulgence. Held in containers which are lavishly decorated with gold, beads and gemme mosaic, jewel-like flowers glow amid dark foliage.

pretty romantics

Light and frilly planting coupled with simple containers makes this collection easy to live with. The idyllic charm of endearing cottage garden plants or dainty flowers has a feminine, romantic feel.

contemporary

Characterized by strong shapes, these containers have a stark simplicity. Made from materials found in contemporary gardens, such as stone, plastics and metal, they have a strong and very modern presence.

ections

passion & daring

Bold and demanding, the containers in this collection are audacious show-stoppers. A daring use of colour seizes the attention, creating drama and energy. These pots make strong features with great personality.

cool sophistication

Controlled and pared down, these containers have a chic restraint. Elegant plants and pots combine in sophisticated good taste. With cool colours and uncluttered planting, they have an air of refinement.

sun-baked mediterranean

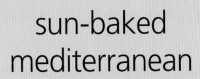

Evocative of clear blue skies and olive groves, these containers evoke a Mediterranean spirit. Terracotta and decorated pots conjure up the warmth, freedom and fragrance of the region.

opulence & riches

purple mosaic trough

Shot with the glitter of gold, gemme mosaic tesserae are wonderfully luxurious – the flecks of precious metal glisten from within the translucent glass tiles. Here a sturdy trough has been embellished with a mosaic of these splendid purple tiles and equally splendid purple paint. The mosaic is quick and simple to apply as the tiles have only been used on the flat faces of the trough, creating a hard-wearing surface which will withstand the worst extremes of the elements. The richly coloured, heavy trough would work well on a windowledge or as the centrepiece on a large rectangular dining table.

ABOVE Held high on seemingly fragile stems, the blooms of the primula will last for several weeks in the early summer, giving height to the display before the vibrant mimulus reach their best.

LEFT & RIGHT An exuberant combination of deep orange mimulus and the clear purple of *Primula capitata mooreana* is a good choice for a lightly shaded location as the strong colours will intensify in the low light. The perennial primula has semi-evergreen foliage and can remain in the trough as part of next summer's display.

FAR RIGHT Exquisitely hot and rich, the orange of the mimulus flowers contrasts beautifully with the purple of the trough.

what to do

1 *Seal a flat-sided terracotta trough, inside and out, with a coat of PVA. You could use a plastic trough if you use a flexible outdoor tile cement and a suitable primer.*

2 *When the PVA is dry, paint the rim and the foot of the trough with purple paint (see page 128). You may need two coats to get a good coverage without the terracotta showing through.*

3 *Cut out sheets of the gemme mosaic tiles to fit the flat panels of the trough as closely as possible.*

4 *Apply a bed of outdoor tile cement to the trough and press the sheets of tiles into place.*

5 *When the cement is dry, spread outdoor tile grout over the surface of the tiles, pushing it into the gaps between them. Polish off the excess grout with a cloth and allow to dry. For further instructions on how to apply mosaic, see page 134.*

LEFT & BELOW This sumptuous purple planting will thrive in the hottest spot in the garden. The flowers of the vigorous *Osteospermum* 'Nasinga Purple', with their spoon-shaped petals, scramble up through the frosted, russet-purple ribbons of *Astelia* 'Westland' to great effect. Osteospermums flower all summer and into the autumn, so long as the spent blooms are removed. Both plants can be kept for the following year in a frost-free environment.

RIGHT These winter pansies will provide a reliable show throughout the winter months and into the spring. The trough will require deadheading regularly, and watering even if it rains, especially if you put it on a windowledge.

BELOW With petals seemingly cut from the finest velvet, few blooms can surpass the richness of common-or-garden pansies.

copper box

Transformed by a coat of gold and copper paint, a simple trough becomes something special. Filled with glorious plants whose blooms and foliage also have the glint of precious metals, the trough will add a touch of luxury to any windowledge or dining table. The strong geometric design is easy to create and the plants chosen are unfussy and should produce an abundance of flowers. The bold pansy 'Bronze Beacon' and the evergreen grass *Uncinia uncinata rubra* make an unusual autumn and winter display, while *Osteospermum* 'Serina' and trailing lemon petunias will flourish from spring to early autumn.

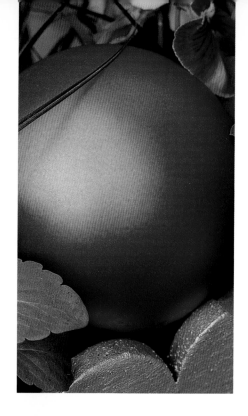

ABOVE Until the trough is lush with foliage and flowers, a copper-coloured glass bauble adds a touch of drama to the composition.

LEFT *Osteospermum* 'Serina' and a yellow trailing petunia will provide a mass of blooms through summer and early autumn. Their contrasting habits add interest to the display. Deadhead regularly to encourage more blooms.

what to do

1 *Seal a terracotta trough with PVA. Paint the trough with gold paint until you achieve an even coverage; it may require two coats.*

2 *Using a ruler and pencil, draw the design on the trough. It does not need to be perfectly accurate.*

3 *Apply two coats of copper paint to the marked areas. Allow the paint to dry before planting. For further instructions on how to paint pots, see page 128.*

BELOW & RIGHT The gold and copper design reflects the kaleidoscope of colour in the pansy 'Bronze Beacon'. The rich velvet blooms nestle among the blades of the grass *Uncinia uncinata rubra* and will bloom from autumn through winter.

beaded hanging pots

Adorned with shining glass beads reminiscent of tiger's eye and amber, these tiny hanging pots are highly decorative and the ideal finishing touch for intimate areas of the garden where their richness and sparkle can be appreciated at close quarters. They can be suspended from the spars of parasols over tables, in trees beside benches, from the beams of pergolas, or in doorways. Hanging like trinkets or baubles on a Christmas tree, the pots are a quick and easy way to brighten these areas, instantly adding another layer of interest to the garden. The pots are very small and will dry out easily, so regular watering is essential.

LEFT & RIGHT Planted with sturdy dwarf chrysanthemums, a host of beaded pots hangs beside a path from a small tree. The advantage of using such small pots is that they can be hung from frail trees and shrubs. With regular deadheading, the plants should bloom well into the autumn months.

what to do

1 *Thread groups of three or four pretty glass beads on to beading wire, and twist the ends of the wire to hold the beads in place.*

2 *Leave a short distance of bare wire, then add another bunch of beads and twist the wire again to hold them in place. Continue until you have a length of beaded wire that will wrap around a pot three times.*

3 *Wrap the beaded wire around the top of a pot and twist the ends to secure it, forming a bead collar. Attach three lengths of wire at equal intervals around the bead collar, leaving the ends free. Once planted, the pots can be hung by twisting the loose wires around the support.*

LEFT With its papery flowers, *Helianthemum* 'Ben More' will perform well if hung in a sunny location. The flowers appear from late spring through summer. The pots are best hung where they can be seen at close quarters, so both pot and flowers can be appreciated. In autumn, the plants could be planted out in the garden as they are unlikely to survive another season in such a small container.

gilded containers

Nothing conjures up a feeling of wealth and opulence better than gold. A thin layer of gold-coloured metal leaf will elevate any container from the everyday to something splendid. Chose a vessel with a raised ornate design and the effect is magnified. Almost any material can be gilded – including concrete, plastic and terracotta – their personalities concealed and supplanted by the glint of precious metal. Gold containers often work best when the planting has the clarity that comes from using a single species rather than an elaborate, fussy scheme. Small gilded containers shine like rare jewels in a garden, while larger vessels are dramatic, dominating and perhaps a little vulgar in their sumptuousness – they should be used with great care.

LEFT & RIGHT Brilliant as gems, *Crocus tommasinianus* gleam in the spring sunshine from their golden vessel. Planted in autumn, the delicate blooms will provide a colourful display for several weeks in the spring.

what to do

1 *Seal terracotta and porous pots with PVA. Apply a thin, even coat of size and leave to dry.*

2 *Lay a sheet of metal leaf on the pot – it will stick to the size. Repeat until the whole surface is covered. Tears can be repaired, creases smoothed out and gaps filled by adding small pieces of leaf and smoothing them into place.*

3 *Smooth the sheets down with a soft cloth or paintbrush and allow the container to dry.*

4 *Apply a coat of clear exterior vanish to protect the surface and allow to dry. For further instructions on how to gild pots, see page 130.*

ABOVE & RIGHT For colour all year round, the fleshy ruby leaves of this sempervivum are a low-maintenance option that will withstand neglect and drought with good grace. The spiky form provides an effective contrast to the smooth urn.

LEFT Here the reflective gold and ornate swag design of this rotund jar require only the addition of the simplest planting to make an interesting accent. The black leaves of *Aeonium* 'Zwartkop' link with the surrounding planting and contrast perfectly with the gold jar. The aeonium is frost tender but during the colder months the jar is decorative enough to shine out among the dark foliage unplanted.

ABOVE & ABOVE RIGHT
Brightening the dark days of late winter, the double snowdrop *Galanthus nivalis* 'Flore Pleno', with its layers of frilled skirts, is well worth elevating to the table top or windowledge where it can be admired at close quarters.

RIGHT A shallow saucer has been gilded inside to make a decoration for the dining table. The almost-black flowers of the *Clematis* 'Romantika' appear to float in a pool of gold.

gold rim decoration

Sumptuously decorated with warm spicy colours and naive gold designs, these pots have an exotic splendour. Gold is always evocative of luxury; here it is used quite sparingly to transform three plain terracotta pots into something really special. Dark, rich foliage plants are used to complete the lavish effect. In the first grouping, the almost-black, velvety leaves of a *Begonia rex*, the startling variegations of *Phormium* 'Rainbow Jester' and the exotic form of *Aeonium* 'Zwartkop' are combined. The strength of the second planting (see page 50) lies in the use of the same plant in each pot – placed close together the leaves of the phormiums intermingle as if of one larger plant.

LEFT A mulch of golden pebbles is the perfect finishing touch. Choose smooth, rounded pebbles and give them two coats of gold paint.

ABOVE This exotic group will thrive in a sunny spot. In winter, replace the tender aeonium (left) and begonia (centre) with two more phormiums.

what to do

1 *Paint three plain terracotta pots with PVA, diluted with a little water if necessary. Leave them to dry.*

2 *Give each of the pots two coats of paint, leaving them to dry between coats. Remember to paint 15 cm (6 in) down inside the pots.*

3 *When the pots are dry, use a pencil to draw on a simple repeating design around the rim. Use a single pencil line to denote the sweeping brush strokes.*

4 *Using a fine paintbrush, fill in the design with gold paint using confident brush strokes. Do not worry about slight irregularities: they are all part of the hand-painted charm of the design. For further instructions on how to paint pots, see page 128.*

ABOVE Using a set of three pots means that the group can be refreshed by rearranging or replanting any one of its members. Here the golden brown tufts of *Carex comans* bronze form create a tantalizing diaphanous screen above which the glossy leaves of *Aeonium* 'Zwartkop' and phormium appear.

RIGHT Composed of a few bold strokes, the naive patterns do not have to be precise.

LEFT The pinks, reds and bronzes of the variegated leaves of the amazing *Phormium* 'Rainbow Jester' work well with the warm colours of the pots. The colourful strap-like leaves provide year-round interest and are wonderfully animated by even the slightest breeze. The phormiums will grow happily for two or three years before outgrowing the pots.

RIGHT With its finely cut ruby leaves, *Acer palmatum* 'Garnet' is the perfect specimen plant to be singled out for special treatment. Here it is elevated above the surrounding planting in a splendid pot, used alone.

BELOW Although the decoration on the pots follows the same theme, the designs are subtly different to add interest to the group. Further interest is added by using three different shades for the pots themselves.

passion & daring

passion for pink

Shocking pink pots with shocking pink plants irresistibly draw the eye. The strength or power of the colour of pot and plant is amplified and exaggerated by the colour match between the two, colour built on colour to create something daring. Grouping three similar pots together only serves to heighten the effect. This vivacious pink will work well in contrast with pale greys, lilacs, punchy yellows, lime-greens and, of course, among other hot pinks. The gold rim contributes just a sliver of contrast between pot and plant. These bold pots would make a lively addition to a terrace or could be used as a showy focal point.

ABOVE Lasting several weeks, the berries of the evergreen *Gaultheria mucronata* are its main attraction. Once they lose their appeal, the plant can be shuffled into a less prominent position or planted out in the garden. It requires an ericaceous compost.

LEFT This trio in pink is all the more amazing when one considers that it is a winter planting. The rest of the garden may be in winter's drab garb, but these plants are resplendent in their pink raiment. This audacious trio will pep up any corner of the terrace.

RIGHT Kept in a sheltered spot, the spider-like form of this vibrant phormium will look good all year round; removing any damaged leaves at the base will keep it looking tidy. It is the perfect evergreen specimen to provide the backbone of a group of pots to change with the seasons.

what to do

1 *Seal three terracotta pots with PVA, inside and out.*

2 *When the PVA is dry, give the pots two coats of pink paint, allowing the first to dry thoroughly before applying the second.*

3 *Add a band of gold paint, about 2.5 cm (1 in) wide, around the rims of the pots and allow to dry. For further instructions on how to paint pots, see page 128.*

LEFT & BELOW Crowded for maximum impact, the blooms of *Tulipa humilis* Violacea Group 'Black Base' jostle for space among the lime-green and yellow blades of *Acorus gramineus* 'Ogon'. The lime-green is a perfect accent colour for this pinkest of plantings. The tulips flower in April from bulbs planted in the previous autumn; they can be planted directly in the pot or grown in flowerpots and transplanted before they bloom. After flowering, the bulbs can be transferred to the garden for next year.

red & black jar

Bold and brilliant, this ample black and red jar demands attention. A pot that makes such a dramatic statement makes a highly successful focal point; it cannot fail to draw the eye. Here colour has been carefully orchestrated to achieve maximum impact: the black and red decoration echoes the colour scheme of the surrounding planting and hardscaping materials, creating a strong coherent scene. The bold choice of colours makes this a love-it or hate-it design, but it can be successfully replicated in any two colours to suit its location and function. Potting up a number of large plastic pots which neatly fit the neck of the jar will allow you to change the planting easily with the seasons.

LEFT & ABOVE Placed at the end of a vista paved with black glass, among vibrant red lilies and dahlias, the portly jar makes an imposing focal point. The huge, red-painted lion's paw pot stands are a witty touch. So striking is the container that a relatively plain planting of *Ophiopogon planiscapus* 'Nigrescens' is just enough, its black strap-like leaves, so often lost against compost, gain prominence against the red rim of the pot. Snipping off dead and damaged leaves will keep the evergreen ophiopogon looking good all year round.

what to do

1 *Seal a large terracotta jar with PVA. A large plastic pot could easily be used instead, and would be lighter to move.*

2 *When the PVA is dry, give the jar a coat of red paint, aiming for an even coverage. Add a second coat if necessary, after allowing the first coat to dry thoroughly.*

3 *Once the paint is dry, use a pencil to mark the triangular design around the neck of the jar.*

4 *Finally, paint the triangles in black. It is easier to do this freehand rather than masking off the area, and the odd wobble really won't matter. For further instructions on how to paint pots, see page 128.*

ABOVE & RIGHT The sheer exuberance of the voluptuous and heavily scented 'Rococo' tulip is a fair match for the painted jar. Neither dominates the scene.

hot fantasy marble

Wild and wayward, this unusual urn will never be part of the chorus line – it is a star performer, a show-stopper. Used wisely, it has the power to lift the garden from the everyday and push at the boundaries of what is expected. It is a theatrical centrepiece with energy and pizzazz for those who want something daring and different. The juxtaposition of the very traditional urn and the unlikely paint effect is all part of the surprise, though the same finish could be used on any container – larger pots will produce the most stunning effects.

ABOVE Though one of a crowd, the marbled urn still steals the show. The urn is planted with an eclectic mix of plants – paprika-red *Achillea* 'Walther Funcke', *Canna* 'Tropicana' with its dark decorative leaves, and the strident *Gazania* 'Gazoo'.

LEFT The large flowers of the *Gazania* are a triumphant display of appealingly combined colours.

what to do

1 Clean and prime a plastic urn using a suitable plastic primer. Apply two coats of cream acrylic paint.

2 Mix a little yellow acrylic paint with scumble glaze and, using a large round brush, roll the paint in an irregular diagonal direction around the pot.

3 Next use a short-bristled brush to stipple the paint and blur the edges of the strokes.

4 Repeat the last two steps using a red acrylic paint. Use the stippling brush to work the paints into each other to create an orange shade.

5 Finally, using a small paintbrush and a rolling action, create irregular veins running through the marble using red paint. For further instructions on how to create a marble effect, see page 132.

BELOW Hot spicy colours characterize the planting in the group. The smaller containers in the arrangement work subtly and sympathetically to show off the star – the urn in the centre.

ABOVE The poppy plants throw up flowers in a range of smouldering colours from orange through to pale yellow.

LEFT A blazing combination of orange and golden-brown mirrors the fiery paint effect of the urn. A riot of orange *Papaver nudicaule* Gartenzwerg Group and mimulus glows like burning coals around the central fountain of *Carex buchananii.* The perennial poppies will flower all summer, dying back to return the following year, while the evergreen carex will remain all through the winter. This planting will tolerate a lightly shaded spot.

RIGHT Resplendent against a lime-green backdrop, the zesty orange of *Coreopsis grandiflora* 'Early Sunrise' is given a lift by its electric-blue companion *Delphinium* 'Delfix'. A skirt of lime-green golden marjoram can be kept cut back – its only purpose is to provide a link between the taller plants and the pot, hiding unattractive stems and compost.

LEFT *Delphinium* 'Delfix' is a true, clear blue which combines well with the orange of the urn, creating a lively contrast.

mosaic tubes

Containers don't have to be oversized to create a spectacle. These two mosaic-covered pipes enliven the border with their interesting form and a startling, yet effective, use of contrasting colours. The diminutive tubes can be moved into an area of planting to spice up those inevitable and unavoidable dull moments, or they could be a permanent feature, punctuating the border with something provocative. Any coloured mosaic tiles could be used to suit the backdrop. Here a pair of tubes is used, flouting the rule which states you should always use groups of three or five. However, a cluster of three or more would be just as effective.

LEFT & ABOVE Set against a backdrop of the lime-green leaves of Bowles' golden sedge (*Carex elata* 'Aurea'), the red tubes planted with trailing red petunias gain prominence from a startling yet pleasing contrast in colour. The annual petunias will bloom abundantly all summer if the spent blooms are snipped off regularly.

what to do

1 *Use a hacksaw to cut two lengths from an 11 cm (4¹/₂ in) diameter plastic pipe. One should be 23 cm (9 in) long, and the other 30 cm (12 in).*

2 *Roll a sheet of mosaic tiles around the pipes, marking and cutting it to fit. Allow the mosaic tiles to stand a few millimetres proud of the top of the pipe to hide the edge. If the fit around the pipe is not exact, use a tile cutter to cut some tiles to fill the gap.*

3 *Mix some outdoor tile cement with an additive to make it flexible. Spread a layer of the cement all around the pipe.*

4 *Once again, roll the mosaic tiles around the tube and push them gently into place. Slot in the cut tiles to fill any gap.*

5 *When the cement is dry, spread white outdoor tile grout over the surface of the mosaic, pushing it into the gaps between the tiles. Polish it off the tiles with a soft cloth.*

6 *Line the tubes with stout plastic sheeting or bags before planting up. For further instructions on how to apply mosaic, see page 134.*

ABOVE Yellow and red always make a fresh combination. Backed by lime-green, its neighbour on the colour wheel, the yellow flowers of *Bidens* 'Yellow Breeze' have a rousing edge that is heightened by the true red of the blooms of their companion, a trailing verbena.

black & gold urn

With a coat of black gloss paint and a spattering of gleaming gold, this heavy, inexpensive concrete urn becomes something splendidly theatrical. The solidity of the urn and its dramatic embellishment endow it with all the presence required of a star performer. The urn makes an irresistible focal point or can be used as a very decorative flourish where the garden needs a lift. It is not a good mixer and is best appreciated alone, or perhaps as one of a matching pair or a lavish string of identical urns marking a path or boundary with sensational grandeur.

LEFT & ABOVE Brimming with exotic 'Yellow Flair' lilies, this planting is not long lasting but has tremendous appeal. The lilies can be planted in pots in the autumn and only put on display when the buds are forming. It may sound labour intensive but having three pots planted and ready to slip into place at the appropriate time is very little trouble, and the pot of lilies and cornus can be reused for several seasons. If that does not appeal, then buy the lilies in bud from a garden centre.

LEFT Zesty and full of vigour, the punch of this lively mix of orange and yellow is increased by being planted in this glossy black urn – the already bright colours are made more conspicuous by the contrast. With a little deadheading and a sunny spot, the bidens and gazania will keep up this spirited performance all summer long.

RIGHT The golden stems of *Cornus stolonifera* 'Flaviramea' make an unusual, dramatic winter display. Set off perfectly by the glossy blackness of the urn, their smooth gold stems glow in the winter sunlight, echoing the gold decoration. Exhibited in this way the real beauty of these superb winter stems is readily seen. In early spring when the leaves begin to open, cut the cornus back hard and transplant it into the garden or keep in a holding area ready for returning to the urn the following autumn.

what to do

1 *Paint an ornate concrete urn with outdoor gloss paint, applying a second coat if necessary, after the first has dried. With the correct primer, you could also use a plastic urn.*

2 *When the black paint is dry, use a small brush to spatter the urn with gold paint. Generously load the brush and tap it sharply against your finger. Stand back regularly while you work to decide where you need more paint. For further instructions on how to paint pots, see page 128.*

passion & daring **65**

cool sophistication

monochrome vases

A sleek, sculptural shape and a coat of matt paint give these vases a crisp, modern elegance. In their naked terracotta they were interesting but unrefined and earthy. A simple coat of white paint has transformed them into something chic, while a contrasting black planting scheme furthers the theme. Any similar pot or even a pipe could be treated in the same way. The planting for this type of container is almost incidental – it is the elegance of the vases used singly or in groups that dominates. These containers are perfect for adding a touch of panache to a calm, understated outdoor space.

LEFT & RIGHT Almost black at its margins, fading to purple at the centre, *Viola* 'Black Jack' is one of the darkest violas, though 'Molly Sanderson' would do just as well. Happy in sun or light shade these violas guarantee a wealth of flowers all summer if they are deadheaded regularly.

what to do

1 *Seal three terracotta vases with PVA, diluted with a little water if necessary, inside and out. Allow to dry thoroughly.*

2 *Give each vase two coats of outdoor matt white paint, allowing the first to dry before applying the second. For further instructions on how to paint pots, see page 128.*

LEFT There is no reason why all the glitter of Christmas should be kept in the house. Bright white sticks and strings of crystal beads make a fitting display for the festive season or for a celebration, and these pots are the obvious choice to house them.

ABOVE With a tousled mass of black strap-like leaves, *Ophiopogon planiscapus* 'Nigrescens' is an obvious choice for these elegant tubes. Offering perhaps the blackest of foliage, the ophiopogon will look good all year round with little effort.

topiary chic

Crisp clipped shapes fashioned from yew, box, bay or privet have a timeless appeal. While some shapes can be rather whimsical, the geometric forms – spheres, cones and cubes – are rather more stylish, making them the perfect choice when dressing a chic area of the garden. The unchanging nature of topiary forms makes them an ideal choice for those containers that form part of the permanent structure of the garden. Here a subtle, broken yellow paint finish shows off the lush green of the foliage of box and bay, while the height of the containers endows the plants with a greater presence (imagine the same small topiary specimens in containers 30 cm/12 in tall). The containers are an inexpensive, light and durable galvanized metal, but the same paint effect could be used on plastic, terracotta or concrete.

RIGHT An imposing trio, here the containers are planted with a bay tree (*Laurus nobilis*), flanked by two box spheres (*Buxus*), creating a dignified display. This group would soften an expanse of wall or act as a focal point.

1

2

3

4

5

6

what to do

1 *Prime the three metal containers with red oxide primer, aiming for an even coverage, and allow to dry.*

2 *Give each container two coats of cream paint, allowing the first to dry before applying the second.*

3 *Place a little light yellow, golden yellow and beige water-based acrylic paints on a tray or old plate.*

4 *Add a little water and mix the colours slightly so you have a mottled paint with streaks of different shades.*

5 *Paint this colourwash over the cream containers so the colours are unevenly distributed across the surface.*

6 *Use a soft cloth to dab over the containers, softening the effect and blurring the brush marks. Finally, when the paint is dry, add a coat of exterior varnish. For further instructions on how to paint pots, see page 128.*

LEFT Used as a pair, the buxus spheres have more of a contemporary chic. As topiary subjects are likely to be in their containers for some time they should be planted in a good loam-based compost.

ABOVE & RIGHT The bare winter stems of *Acer palmatum* 'Sango-kaku' make a colourful yet elegant subject for a winter planting. The summer leaves will make the overall effect less graphic, but still elegant nonetheless. A mulch of crushed shells sets off the red stems of the acer beautifully.

pewtered urns

With the sheen of polished pewter, these impressive urns make a bold but distinguished statement. Restrained, simple planting helps foster a sophisticated mood. The metallic shine of the pewter paint effect is very eye catching; this, coupled with their size, makes the urns a stylish choice for a focal point or as sentries flanking other garden features such as benches or entrances. The easiest way to plant a monumental urn is to have a series of plastic pots which fit neatly inside the urn, so that plants can be changed to suit the season without too much fuss.

LEFT & ABOVE Container plantings for Christmas are fun. Here a blue spruce Christmas tree with a sprinkling of silver decorations conjures up the festive season outdoors. The live tree can be planted out or potted on and pressed into service again next year.

what to do

1 *Apply a coat of suitable primer to a clean container. Allow to dry thoroughly.*

2 *Next give the container a coat of dark grey paint. Allow the paint to dry then add a second coat and allow to dry again.*

3 *Work gilding cream onto the raised areas of the container to make highlights, fading the silver cream into the grey paint. For further instructions on how to achieve a pewter effect, see page 135.*

LEFT When they are in full bloom, rhododendrons make interesting container subjects for a lightly shaded position. The white flowers of *Rhododendron* 'Alpen Rose' are all the more brilliant for being couched in dark evergreen foliage and set in the grey urn. Provided with ericaceous compost, it will flower over a long period throughout spring.

cool sophistication **75**

RIGHT Resplendent in mid spring, the vigorous *Narcissus* 'Thalia' will produce a profusion of long-lived white flowers with little effort. Simply plant the bulbs in autumn, leave the pot in a sheltered spot and nature should take care of the rest. This simple white planting keeps the power of this dramatic urn restrained, confirming its elegance. A group of silvered glass balls in the top of the urn just lifts the composition.

LEFT & ABOVE A froth of white and silver fills the urn for the summer months, the pure whites radiant in the summer sun. The spiny silver of *Eryngium variifolium* provides the central focus of the planting, while *Convolvulus cneorum* provides bulk. The lustrous white flowers of *Nemesia* 'Natalie Improved' and nierembergia form a cloud of white. The perennials in the display can remain in the container for a couple of seasons if they are planted in a good loam-based compost.

striped cubes

Smartly striped with pewter and white paint, plain terracotta boxes take on an air of sophistication. The striped decoration is easy to apply and could be used to give a cosmopolitan feel to any pot with a simple strong form. As a group of three, the cubes would contribute to the flair of a sleek, crisp terrace or add style arranged along a stretch of gravelled path or wall. A mulch of chunky, peppered granite cobbles takes the colour theme right up to the stems of the plant, linking plant to pot and contributing an interesting texture.

RIGHT A stalwart of winter containers, *Skimmia japonica* 'Rubella' benefits from standing alone; the pleasing shape of the shrub and the prominence of its ruby buds are lost in the mayhem of a mixed planting. Here its simple qualities can be fully appreciated.

FAR RIGHT Arranged against a rendered white wall, this smart threesome is planted with muted tones. The evergreen *Skimmia japonica* 'Rubella', with its clusters of dark red buds, is flanked by two wonderful specimens of *Cornus alba* 'Kesselringii' with stark smooth stems that go from black to a rich mahogany. Both of these plants are best in winter, and both lose their star quality once spring arrives, so replace the display.

what to do

1 *Seal each terracotta cube with PVA, inside and out, and allow it to dry. Give each cube two coats of white paint, allowing the first to dry before applying the second, making sure you achieve an even coverage. Allow to dry thoroughly.*

2 *Use low-tack masking tape to mask off the areas of the pot that are to remain white. Paint the stripes on the unmasked area using a pewter-coloured paint. When the paint is completely dry, carefully remove the tape to reveal the crisp-edged stripes. For further instructions on how to paint pots, see page 128.*

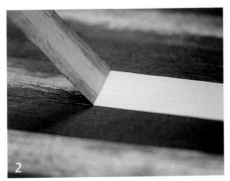

LEFT With an easy sophistication, the pure white blooms of the rhododendron 'Alpen Rose' glisten among dark green leathery foliage for a long period in spring. The rhododendron could be the full-time occupant of the cube for several years, the glossy foliage providing a constant presence all year round. Alternatively, the shrub could be replaced and moved to a holding area until the following spring. To keep the rhododendron looking its best, plant it in ericaceous compost and remove the spent blooms.

RIGHT An unusual choice for a container, *Rubus thibetanus* is a specimen at its most interesting in the winter months when a silvery white bloom reminiscent of frost coats its mahogany-red stems. In spring when the skeletal stems are clothed with delicate grey-green leaves, the bramble can be planted out into the garden or relegated to a holding area until next year. For the best growth, cut to the ground after fruiting. Take care when handling the plant as the cool white bloom is easily rubbed from the spiny stems.

silver chic

Smooth, sleek and shining, a layer of silver leaf applied to a container with clean lines will transform it into the perfect chic decorative feature. If the container is overly ornate, the elegant simplicity is lost. White planting complements the silver finish perfectly and continues the mood – the reflective qualities of the gilded container and white blooms bring a brightness to the garden. Almost any type of container can be gilded – the personalities of plastic, terracotta and concrete are all easily concealed under a slick skin of imitation silver.

ABOVE RIGHT A brilliant array of white blooms fills the trough for summer – marguerites, stocks, osteospermum and verbena, staples of summer planting, will keep up this show into the early autumn. Remove the dead heads regularly to keep the planting tidy and encourage more flowers.

RIGHT Incandescent in the late winter sun, a host of glowing crocus 'White Beauty' froths out of the silver trough. For a good display, disregard recommended planting distances and fill the container with as many bulbs as possible. The effect will be far more impressive. Planted in pots in the autumn, the bulbs will look after themselves and can be moved into the trough before they flower.

what to do

1 *Seal a terracotta trough with PVA and allow to dry. Apply a coat of size and allow to dry again.*

2 *Lay a sheet of metal left on the trough and stick in place. Repeat until the whole surface is covered. Smooth the sheets down using a soft cloth or paintbrush and allow to dry.*

3 *Give the container a coat of clear exterior vanish to protect the surface. For further instructions on how to gild containers, see page 130.*

ABOVE & RIGHT Sprouting from a mass of fragrant thyme, the starburst blooms of *Allium schubertii* provide a surprising display in early summer. Both plants should be planted in autumn. The leaves of alliums can be damaged by wind and rain, spoiling the look of the planting, so here they have been cut back below the thyme.

pretty romantics

blue glass pots

Encrusted with sparkling chips of blue glass, tiny inexpensive terracotta or plastic pots really show off small plants, making a big impact out of a few basic elements. The same technique could be used to disguise unattractive recycled containers or even brighten up the pots in which the plants are bought. Applying the glass mulch is a simple process that hardly takes any time at all. Glass mulch is available in many different colours, but this vivid blue will set off a whole range of colourful plants.

RIGHT Brightly coloured and floriferous violas make excellent occupants for small pots. The viola 'Penny Orange' will provide a good display over many months if it is deadheaded.

what to do

1 *Working a section at a time, squeeze some silicone sealant onto the pot.*

2 *Use an old table or palate knife to spread it into an even layer.*

3 *Tip some glass mulch onto a tray and roll the pot in the mulch until the pot is covered, tucking in extra pieces to fill spaces. Leave to dry.*

LEFT The vivid blue of the pot brings out the delicate blue-green of the fleshy leaves of *Echeveria peacockii*. Succulents such as this will thrive in a small pot if planted in gritty compost with good drainage.

BELOW LEFT Three red imitation gerbera flowers make an amusing and sculptural composition at any time of year.

BELOW Three tousled mops of *Festuca glauca* 'Elijah Blue' make an unusually pretty trio appreciative of a sunny spot. Alone in a plain pot, the grass would not look nearly so engaging, but these three make an attractive decoration for a windowledge or tabletop.

baskets & buckets

If your aim is to conjure up the ambience and rural charm of a cottage garden or country retreat, baskets and buckets brimming with pretty flowers will do the trick. Easily adapted to hold compost, these readily available containers have a home-spun, wholesome feel. Junk shops are usually littered with baskets that will fit the bill – anything from a fruit basket to a log basket can be planted up with pretty flowers to achieve the carefree country mood. Equally, inexpensive galvanized buckets given a distressed paint finish have an uplifting, pastoral charm. Arrange baskets or buckets of different sizes in informal groups to add to the relaxed style.

To prepare a basket for planting, simply line it with a robust plastic bag or sack and pierce drainage holes in the base. Dark-coloured bags are better as they will not show through the weave of the basket. If you want to prolong the life of the basket, give it two coats of yacht varnish. Without such protection the basket should last a year or two.

RIGHT A flourish of crinkled foliage spilling out of the weather-worn bucket makes a simple but effective container planting, and since these leaves belong to lettuces they are fast growing and edible too.

LEFT This blue and yellow combination of blue *Anemone blanda* and crocus 'Goldilocks' has the unkempt appeal and informality of wild flowers. The bulbs and corms need to be planted densely in the bucket in autumn to achieve this look. When the flowers fade, the bulbs can be left there to bloom the following season.

what to do

1 *To decorate a galvanized bucket, first give the bucket a coat of metal primer. When this is dry, apply two coats of light blue paint, allowing the first to dry before applying the second.*

2 *Next rub a wax candle over the prominent areas of the bucket. This acts as a resist and stops the next coat of paint from adhering properly.*

3 *Now apply one or two coats of a buttery yellow paint, again leaving the bucket to dry between coats.*

4 *Use fine sand paper to rub over the prominent areas again – the yellow paint should rub off to leave a worn, shabby look. For further information on how to paint pots, see page 128.*

LEFT Nothing can be prettier or more romantic than blossom time. Here the spirit of blossom-covered orchards has been distilled. A tiny *Prunus incisa* 'Kojo-no-mai' provides blossom a-plenty, if in miniature. A mulch of crushed shells in the top of the pot could be mistaken for fallen blossom.

ABOVE & RIGHT Bright and cheery, this perky combination of pinks and yellows contains the essence and promise of the best days of spring. The robust narcissus 'Tête-a-Tête' is underplanted with primulas with just a little *Acorus gramineus* 'Ogon' contributing an interesting contrast in texture. The baskets sit harmoniously, in colour and style, against a rustic yellow fence or on a blue table. Narcissus bulbs can be planted in pots in autumn, although this type of planting is easily created instantly with plants in bud from the garden centre.

ABOVE A staple of spring containers, primulas come in a range of forceful colours, a blessing if they are used with thought, but not so if the colours are randomly planted together producing a jarring, cacophonous arrangement. Here you only have to look at the centre of the primula to divine a suitable partner.

ABOVE Charmingly petite, yet a reliably good performer, the diminutive narcissus 'Tête-à-Tête' is a good choice for small containers.

ABOVE RIGHT A cottage garden favourite, sweet williams nestled in a small basket make a deliciously fragrant container. This is simple but very effective.

RIGHT The shaggy daisy flowers of *Bellis perennis* 'Pomponette' are entirely suited to this unsophisticated style.

seaside stripes

Redolent of the romance of seaside beach huts and holidays, brightly coloured stripes are perhaps the simplest design for a painted pot. Small, square pots striped with yellow and blue are quick and easy to make and will brighten up tables, terraces and windowledges. A mulch of crushed seashells not only links pot to plant, obscuring dark compost, but continues the subtle seaside theme.

ABOVE Using well-chosen props around a container can give it greater presence. These plain marble spheres mirror the colours around them, making a basic planting of *Koeleria glauca* into something more conspicuous.

LEFT In an irresistible sunshine and blue-skies combination, the bright and breezy yellow flowers of a gerbera contrast harmoniously with the blue striped pot. Regular deadheading will ensure there is always a good show of flowers.

what to do

1 *Seal three terracotta pots with PVA. Apply two coats of cream paint, allowing the first to dry before applying the second.*

2 *Use low-tack masking tape to mark out the stripes, and paint them with blue or yellow paint (see page 79). When the paint is dry gently remove the tape. In this case the stripes need not be crisp, so you could paint them freehand if you prefer. For further information on how to paint pots, see page 128.*

ABOVE LEFT Succulents have a real seaside feel and make perfect tenants for small containers. They demand little attention except protection from frosts.

ABOVE A mulch of crushed shells shows off the plant's foliage and provides a visual link between pot and plant.

LEFT Easy and straightforward but very effective – yellow primulas in butterscotch yellow pots. Both plants and pot gain from the partnership.

blue marbled pots

Pretty does not have to be sickly sweet. Refreshingly cool and snappy, these fantasy marble pots are undoubtedly pretty. The crisp blues and whites of the painted decoration are tempered by fragile and delicate blooms which soften the overall effect to produce something charming. Harsher, jagged planting would produce quite a different feel. Blue is a recessive colour which can be lacking in spirit, but teamed with white it is bright and lively. These medium-sized pots are very versatile and could be used on the terrace, doorstep or perhaps next to a bench. Of course the same technique could be used to decorate pots of any size, although very large vessels may be startling rather than pretty.

RIGHT A frothy display of summery, choice flowers in white and blue mirror the colour of the marbled pot so that both gain from the association – imagine the same planting in a plain terracotta pot; it would not be nearly so lively. The seemingly insignificant sunshine yellow centres of the cosmos and *Nierembergia scoparia* 'Mont Blanc' give the combination a lift by adding a touch of warmth.

what to do

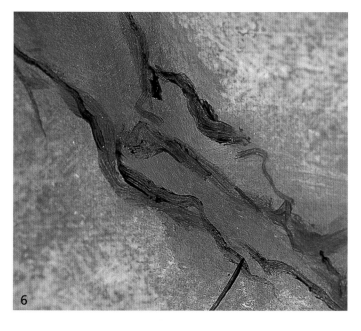

6

1 *Clean and seal three terracotta pots with PVA. If you choose plastic containers, use a suitable primer instead.*

2 *When the sealant is dry, apply two coats of white acrylic paint, allowing the first to dry before applying the second.*

3 *Mix a little light blue acrylic paint with some scumble glaze and, using a large round paintbrush, roll it in an irregular diagonal direction around the pot.*

4 *Next use a short-bristled brush to stipple out the paint, blurring the edges of the brush strokes.*

5 *Now repeat steps 3 and 4 with a darker blue paint. Use the stippling brush to work the two colours into each other and produce a more mellow effect.*

6 *Finally, use a small paintbrush and a rolling action to create irregular veins running through the marble. For further instructions on how to create a marble effect, see page 132.*

ABOVE When seen against a lime-green backdrop, the rich blue blooms of *Delphinium* 'Delphix' gain in intensity.

LEFT With regular deadheading, the white cosmos will produce its jaunty open flowers all through the summer months.

LEFT & BELOW In the gloomiest of winter light, the white blooms of winter-flowering heather and cyclamen will shine out, providing a welcome bright spot on dark days. The marbled pattern of the cyclamen leaves echoes that of the pot.

LEFT Gleaming white hyacinths, with their towers of bell-like blooms, not only make a pretty spectacle but produce the most seductively pretty smell. Crammed five to a pot, three pots in a row, the blooms make a sensational display that is unsentimentally pretty and immensely fragrant. Their sweet scent would make a wonderful greeting on a doorstep.

pretty in pink

Lively, agreeable and positive, pink is the colour of prettiness. Here the more sugar-sweet shades have been passed over, as exquisite flowers in strong pinks produce a more contemporary take on pretty. Single plants are offered up for close inspection in small rotund jars so their vivacious charms can be appreciated. The success of this arrangement belies its lack of expense and the speed at which it can be achieved. The bulbous jars lend a great deal of character but straight-sided flowerpots would work well with the same paint treatment.

RIGHT The skyward-reaching spikes of winter-flowering heather, clothed in the pinkest of pink bells, continue the theme through the darkest months of the year. Heathers need little care except the provision of an ericaceous compost.

what to do

1 *Clean and seal three terracotta pots with PVA and allow to dry.*

2 *Apply two coats of lilac paint to each of the pots, allowing the first coat to dry before applying the second.*

3 *When this is dry, paint a pink rim around the neck of the pots. For further instructions on how to paint pots, see page 128.*

ABOVE & ABOVE LEFT *Armeria maritima* 'Nifty Thrifty' throws up a host of pink bauble-like flowers on wiry stems all through the summer. Through the rest of the year, it caps the jar with a mop of lime-green, grass-like leaves. The evergreen leaves may not have the same allure as the plant in bloom, but the interesting shapes are enough to make it work.

LEFT Held on stiff stems above gently marbled foliage, the fluttering, butterfly-like blooms of *Cyclamen* 'Miracle' give an animated performance in early spring. These hard-working little plants will produce plenty of flowers in a sunny or semi-shaded spot.

contemporary

lead wraps

Unadorned lead cylinders make the perfect contemporary cachepot to exhibit a single plant. The dull grey metal develops a soft white bloom over time that complements a myriad of plants. The plainness and simplicity of the robust tubes will leave the eye with no choice but to concentrate on the intricacies of the plants. This is perhaps container gardening at its most convenient – inexpensive plants bought from the garden centre at their peak are merely slipped into the tubes, still in their pots, and replaced once they fade. This means it is possible to have a special display on a windowledge or tabletop at all times, and probably at less cost than cut flowers. The lead wraps are simple to make and the same technique could be used for larger pots.

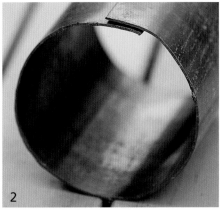

what to do

1 *You will need a length of 13.5 cm (5^1/$_2$ in) lead roll, used for roofing. Wearing gloves, roll the length of lead around a plastic pipe with a diameter of about 11 cm (4^1/$_2$ in).*

2 *Use tin snips to cut off the lead wrap, leaving an overlap of about 2.5 cm (1 in). Slide out the plastic pipe and the lead wrap will hold its shape.*

3 *Simply slip a potted plant inside the lead collar and the display is complete.*

LEFT & BELOW The striking forms of small succulents make them perfect for plain containers. Dusted with a grey bloom, the thick, crinkly, pink-edged leaves of *Cotyledon undulata* associate well with the matt grey of the lead.

LEFT Surrounded by glossy evergreen leaves, the bright red berries of *Skimmia japonica reevsiana* make it a favourite for winter container schemes. Here held in a lead wrap, the plants are given room to look their best. The aim is to achieve a contemporary simplicity.

ABOVE Held high on downy stems, the fresh white blooms of *Primula denticulata alba* will persist over several weeks in early to mid spring. The pure white flowers are perfect for brightening a shady spot, though the plant will do well in sun if its compost is moist.

coil pots

Plants will often live quite happily for some time in the pots they are bought in. However, plastic pots are unattractive and do little to show off the plants. Here such pots are quickly and easily disguised with a wrapping of chain, rope or even rubber tubing. Swathing the pots in these materials is a stylish solution which is completed in an instant. Once in place, the contemporary cloak of ropes and chains requires no fixing and has all the advantages and flexibility of being temporary. Chains produce a harsh, brash container, whereas the loops of rope have a more natural and gentle appeal. Both work well with natural stone and wood although to different effect.

RIGHT Shackled with heavy chains, the spiny *Euphorbia pentagona* looks tough and uncompromising. The gleaming silver chain works well with the grey stone hardscaping and bestows upon the tiny euphorbia a personality and presence it would not otherwise possess. Despite its tough appearance, the euphorbia is not hardy and will only tolerate outdoor life in the warmest months of the year.

RIGHT Harsh reflective metal containers are much favoured in contemporary gardens, and a simple, heavy length of chain is all you need for an inexpensive and stylish example.

what to do

1 *Wind a length of chain or rope around a plant pot to cover it. Chain and rope will stay in place of their own accord. When using a chain with large links, it is possible that small glimpses of the underlying pot may still be visible. If the plant is small, repot it into an empty tin furnished with drainage holes for a better effect.*

LEFT Even the prettiest of little flowers, like *rhodohypoxis*, can be given a contemporary edge. The juxtaposition of dainty pink flowers and hefty chain is fun.

ABOVE Soft rubber gas tubing has been coiled up to make a quirky container for a spiky *Festuca glauca*. The springy tube is held in place with wire twisted from one coil to the next.

ABOVE Coiled around the pot, the loops of rope sit neatly on top of each other so the pot is entirely covered.

LEFT The architectural forms of grasses and sedges make them a good choice for modern containers. Here a fountain of wispy golden brown strands, seemingly held together by a binding of rope, has an easiness and warmth. The rope and the *Carex* are in complete harmony and almost seem to be spun from the same material.

RIGHT A more lavish coil of rope has a less uniform, contrived appearance. This casual arrangement of rope and aloe looks relaxed, as if it just happened.

BELOW *Cycas revoluta* has an almost seaside feel in its rope-covered pot. It will thrive in a sunny spot outside during the summer, but will need to be taken inside before colder weather arrives – it will only withstand temperatures down to 13°C (55°F).

stone cubes

With a solidity and permanence that comes from being hewn from solid rock, these hefty stone cubes have a masculine, rugged edge. Plain and natural, the stone is left to speak for itself, its striations and pigmentations providing interest enough. Cleverly constructed from square slate floor tiles, these cubes are easy to make and can either be used as a cachepot, or lined with stout polythene and planted up in the usual way.

what to do

1 *Choose four 30 cm (12 in) slate floor tiles. Use a pencil to mark the positions of four holes on each tile, two on each of two opposite sides. Mark one hole 5 cm (2 in) from the top of each side and the other 5 cm (2 in) from the bottom.*

2 *Use a masonry bit on an electric drill to create the holes as marked.*

3 *Join the four tiles together to form a box by threading a thick wire through the pairs of holes and twisting it to make it secure. The cube will lack rigidity until it is in position and planted.*

RIGHT Architectural fronds possessed by most ferns make them great subjects for contemporary containers where a bold simplicity reigns. This stout *Polystichum* fern suits the sturdy slate container and will thrive in difficult shady areas.

FAR LEFT & RIGHT The robust slate cubes sit happily among other natural materials. Here a mulch of the same gravel it sits upon gives it a link with its surroundings. This *Sciadopitys verticillata* will eventually grow enormous but will happily spend a couple of years in a container this size given a loam-based compost and a lightly shaded spot.

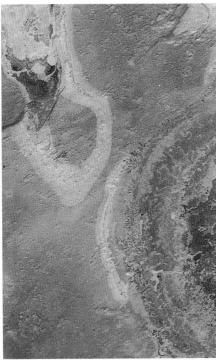

BELOW With all the lush green extravagance of a tropical jungle, *Paulownia tomentosa* has enormous leaves. It is an impressive and unexpected occupant for a container. The plant is both kept small and persuaded to produce its gargantuan leaves by cutting it back extremely hard in the spring. To keep it healthy and vigorous, it should be planted in good loam-based compost.

orange tower

Startling orange sheets of acrylic have been strung together to make a striking, uncompromising container. After dark this container is no less obtrusive, as a spotlight glows through the semi-transparent acrylic, dramatically uplighting the plants. Containers of almost any size or colour could be constructed using the same method. The low-voltage spotlights used to illuminate the tower are easy to fit, but will require a power source that should be installed by a qualified electrician. Acrylic sheet is readily available from plastics retailers.

FAR RIGHT The rich purple leaves of *Sambucus* 'Black Lace' are bold enough to hold their own against this strident orange, and in fact they benefit from the contrast. The robust shrub has a profusion of delicately cut leaves reminiscent of those of an acer, and can be kept compact by cutting back hard in early spring. Perhaps one drawback of this dramatic combination is that the sambucus is deciduous. An evergreen alternative is *Phyllostachys nigra*, an elegant bamboo with jet-black stems.

RIGHT In the twilight, the drama increases as the light illuminates the foliage and glows warmly through the acrylic panels.

what to do

1 *Ask your supplier to cut four pieces of acrylic 37.5 x 100 cm (15 x 40 in).*

2 *Mark the positions of three holes on the two longest sides of each of the sheets. Mark the first holes 20 cm (8 in) from the tops of the sheets, the second holes 20 cm (8 in) from the bottoms of the sheets and the third holes in the middle. Mark the positions of the holes about 2.5 cm (1 in) in from the edges. Make the holes with a wood bit fitted to an electric drill.*

3

3 *Next tie the four panels together. Stand two panels at right angles to each other and pass a length of black cord through the top pair of holes so that the two ends of the cord are on the outside. Tie a knot and pass the ends of the cord back through the same holes to the inside and tie another knot. Continue lacing together pairs of holes until the pieces are joined.*

4 *Place the tower in position and pass the light cable down through the tower and out the bottom.*

5 *Line the tower with a stout plastic sack and pierce drainage holes at the base. Add a layer of pebbles for drainage, and fill the tower with compost to within 20 cm (8 in) of the top.*

6 *Push the spotlight into the compost and the tower is ready for planting.*

5

6

sun-baked

mediterranean

wall of pots

All over the Mediterranean, balconies, walls and terraces are festooned with pots holding a cascade of brightly coloured flowers. This exuberant style is mimicked here by hanging sunny yellow pots from a trellis painted in the same colour, making a display redolent of the Mediterranean's heat and sizzling colours. The trellis will look most authentic set against a south-facing, white-washed wall, or one of rugged stone. As it really only occupies vertical space, the trellis can be used to provide interest in the smallest of gardens or even a balcony.

ABOVE & RIGHT A favourite in the Mediterranean, red pelargoniums thrive in the hottest of hot spots, even in these small elevated pots. The vibrant red flowers sing out boisterously against the yellow of the pots and trellis in an explosion of colour. The geraniums are tender but can be overwintered in a frost-free environment.

what to do

1 Prime and paint an untreated trellis panel with yellow paint. Seal ten plain terracotta pots with PVA and paint them yellow, using two coats if necessary and allowing the first to dry before applying the second. For further instructions on how to paint pots, see page 128.

2 When the pots are dry, use a masonry drill bit to drill two holes about 2 cm (³/4 in) apart just under the rim of each pot.

3 Thread a length of wire through the holes in each pot, leaving the free ends outside the pot.

4 Arrange the pots on the trellis and secure them in place by twisting the wires together around the trellis. Attach the trellis to the wall.

LEFT & BELOW The fiery flowers of *Lantana* will keep up this scorching display from late spring to late autumn on a sunny wall. The plants are frost tender but can be successfully overwintered in a greenhouse or on a windowsill and returned to the garden once the risk of frost has passed in the spring.

recycled tin

In the struggle to fill every corner with flowers and foliage, Mediterranean gardeners often resort to recycled containers to hold plants. It is a great trick which, if done with some élan, is very successful. The tins should have an authentic Mediterranean feel – look in delicatessens or ask in restaurants for unwanted tins.

LEFT & ABOVE In the Mediterranean, plants are often crammed together with fruit, vegetables and flowers side by side in relaxed informality. Here an Ogen melon, with its twining tendrils and lush foliage, shares a container with a scented geranium. The melon is unlikely to bare fruit outside, but its foliage and twining habit are pleasing. The geranium conjures up the warm fragrance of warmer climes.

what to do

1 *Wash out the tin with warm soapy water and allow to dry.*

2 *Use a hammer and a nail to punch a number of drainage holes in the bottom of the tin to allow excess water to drain away. Plant up as normal.*

ABOVE Glamorous and showy cannas make excellent container subjects, boasting striking flowers, ornamental foliage and flowering well into the autumn. This frost-tender plant springs from rhizomes which can be removed and stored in a frost-free environment through the winter.

RIGHT Not strictly a Mediterranean native, the exotically fragrant *Trachelospermum jasminoides* is a popular import. This beautiful climber has many virtues – wonderfully fragrant flowers, neat, glossy evergreen foliage and the ability to climb unaided given a suitable support.

olive grove

Two indisputable symbols of the Mediterranean region are the olive tree and lavender. Together they effortlessly conjure up clear blue skies and the spirit of the region. Planted in plain, squat terracotta pots, a group of five young olive trees underplanted with lavender may lack the gnarled weather-beaten character of ancient olives, but they could not be more evocative of the area. Lavender is a garden favourite, easy going and undemanding. A trim after flowering and again in the spring is all that is required to keep the plants neat. Planting in a good loam-based compost with extra grit and a good provision for drainage should help combat waterlogging.

ABOVE RIGHT Olives have an undeserved reputation for being tender; they will in fact tolerate temperatures as low as −10°C (14°F), but will not survive being waterlogged, especially in cold winter weather.

RIGHT Standing side by side, the pots help to soften this expansive south-facing wall, the long stems of the lavender blooms reaching out towards the sunshine.

ABOVE Arranged around a bench, the planted pots are the only thing needed to create a convincingly Mediterranean feel in this tiny gravel courtyard. The space owes its character to the two plants, simply but effectively presented.

RIGHT On warm days the fragrant lavender blooms are alive with the comforting bustle of bees, butterflies and other insects.

what to do

1 Choose a number of squat, plain terracotta pots with a Mediterranean feel – square or round pots will work just as well as each other.

2 Plant an olive tree in the middle of each of the pots.

3 Surround the olive tree with three or five lavender plants, depending on their eventual size, equally spaced around the edges of the pot.

terracotta

No discussion of Mediterranean container gardening could refrain from expounding the glories of terracotta – warm, natural and shaped from the earth. Whether grand and ancient like the pots furnishing the Biboli gardens or the Villa Garzoni, or smaller and more humble, terracotta, if mellow in tone, is always sympathetic to plants and will stand harmoniously among natural materials. For centuries terracotta has been employed in the Mediterranean, not just to adorn gardens but also to create vital storage vessels, roof tiles, paving and even beehives. Terracotta is adaptable, versatile and immensely practical and possesses the enviable gift of aging with grace. Made from local clays, the qualities, colour and style of pots have great regional variation; many designs and shapes are part of a long tradition that is still evolving.

ABOVE These lemon trees are growing in robust terracotta pots in Tuscany. Pots from the Impruneta region are of superb quality and especially hardy, but beware – other less robust terracotta may shatter or flake in harsh weather conditions.

LEFT The craftsmanship and beauty of the applied decoration on grander pots can be breathtaking.

For a relaxed atmosphere, cram terracotta pots with vibrant, colourful planting. Crowd small pots into sprawling groups, litter walls and line windowsills with them. Use larger olive jars as focal points or to punctuate fragrant Mediterranean plantings. It is worthwhile investing in at least one or two olive or fig trees, or perhaps a citrus or vine, to grow in pots, so characteristic are they of the area. To evoke the more stately charms of the great gardens of the region, choose fewer larger pots and plant them with orange or lemon trees. Arrange pots in rows along crisp gravel paths or walls and use highly decorated urns as focal points.

LEFT The essence of the Italian formal garden, this impressive Impruneta terracotta pot planted with an architectural orange tree is the perfect choice to capture the spirit of grand Mediterranean designs. The orange needs to be protected from harsh weather; the pot however can easily withstand a sharp frost.

sun-baked mediterranean **121**

Whether you crave the exuberant, sun-baked Mediterranean style or the more measured formality of the region's great gardens, using authentic pots from the area will undoubtedly offer the best start. Without planting or staging they will work as they are, after all, the fired earth of the Mediterranean. If you can't get the real thing, select less expensive machine-made pots, imported from other regions of the world. But choose carefully, picking those with a mellow hue, not a brash brick-red or pallid pinky-buff colour, and those with shapes redolent of the region.

ABOVE This Greek-style terracotta pot has a naive charm which is accentuated by the simple lines of the red sempervivum growing in it.

LEFT Growing better with age, terracotta gently mellows. Its edges soften with the passage of time, its surface weathers and it becomes colonized by lichens; in short it becomes part of the landscape. Few other containers can offer such long-lasting appeal.

ABOVE Good-quality terracotta pots proudly display the stamps of their factory or region.

LEFT In such a venerable jar the planting is barely necessary: the carpet of golden blooms gives the pot a gentle lift. A shallow bowl sat in the mouth of the jar makes planting an easy matter. Large jars, planted or unplanted, make atmospheric focal points.

LEFT Perfectly proportioned and frost hardy, these miniature pots, brimming with rich purple aubrieta, have a sun-bleached quality reminiscent of the Mediterranean. A line of such pots could be used to decorate a windowledge, a shelf attached to a courtyard wall, or a rustic dining table.

ABOVE These bulbous egg-shaped pots have a contemporary feel; the repetition of the smooth shapes creates a pleasing, strong effect. The planting of *Fascicularia bicolor* is almost incidental to the display, but stops the line of pots appearing too sterile.

LEFT The traditional moulded relief decorations have an appeal that transcends the whims of fashion.

sun-baked mediterranean **125**

decorative techniques

The following pages contain everything you will need to know to replicate the decorative techniques used in this book. Easily mastered, the techniques offer an almost infinite array of ways to change or mould the personality of a pot. Humble terracotta can become sumptuous with a skin of gold, plastic pots beguile with a mosaic façade and even the simplest painted designs will shape a pot's charms. Following the basic guidelines, the techniques can be adapted to fit your needs, colours changed or patterns altered to reflect the style of your garden – experiment with colours, designs, materials and paints to create something unique.

painting pots

A coat of paint applied to the most ordinary of containers can effect a miraculous transformation. For lasting results, use exterior paint; otherwise you can experiment with all kinds of paint, most of which will last a season or two.

Artists' acrylics offer a fantastic range of colours and tend to fare reasonably well in the garden; standard emulsion, gloss and eggshell paints should last a season or two and even look appealing when they have a slightly worn look; you could even try car spray paints. There are specialist paints made for terracotta, plastic and stone, which should give a quality finish.

To ensure the best chance of longevity for your painted pot, take some time over the preparation. All containers should be absolutely dry; porous materials like terracotta or wood may need drying out for several days in a warm place before painting. The surfaces should be as clean as possible – any rough areas on terracotta and wood or seams on plastic pots can be removed using sand paper.

Next apply an appropriate sealant or base coat. Porous materials can be sealed using PVA. This will prevent moisture permeating the body of the pot. The PVA needs to be thin enough to coat the pot smoothly, so dilute it with a little water if necessary. Metal containers require a coat of red oxide metal primer to prevent rust developing and spoiling the painted surface, and give a good key for the painted decoration. A coat or two of a good wood primer is sufficient for wooden boxes or troughs. The smooth finish of plastic containers makes it hard for paint to adhere to its surface, so use a special plastic primer or the paint will simply peel away.

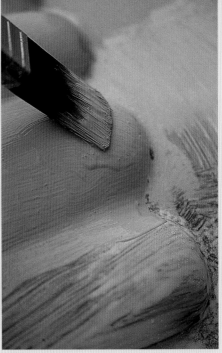

ABOVE A basic terracotta pot has been painted in yellow, with a simple repeating pattern in gold paint on top.

LEFT Metal pots need to be treated with a coat of red oxide primer to prevent rust bubbling through the paint. Apply an even coat, inside and out, following the manufacturer's instructions.

1 *Using an appropriate sealant, coat the container inside and out. Terracotta can be sealed with a smooth, even coat of PVA. Thin the PVA with equal quantities of water, if necessary, so it can be applied more easily.*

2 *Once the sealant is dry, apply a coat of the paint that forms the main part of the design. Again, aim for a smooth, even coverage. Apply a second coat, if necessary, allowing the first coat to dry thoroughly before you do.*

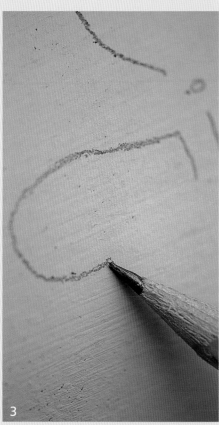

3 *When the paint is dry, use light pencil strokes to mark a design onto the pot. Simple designs often have the most impact and are easier to execute. Once you gain confidence it is much easier to draw freehand.*

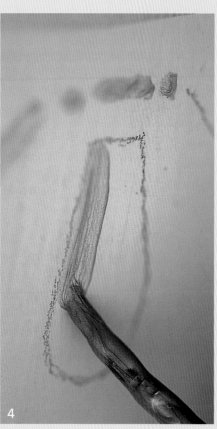

4 *Using a fine paintbrush, fill in the design with confident brush strokes, taking care to cover the pencil marks. Do not worry about irregularities: they are all part of the hand-painted charm. You may need more than one coat of paint, depending on the intensity of the colour. Protect the pot from the elements until it is completely dry.*

gilding

This technique will add the lustre of precious metal to plastic, concrete, stone or terracotta containers. The glamorous results you can achieve with metal leaf belie the ease of application.

There are plenty of different metal leaves available – gold, silver, copper and so on. You can buy the real thing, for example real gold leaf, but the imitations look just as good and are much less expensive as well as being easier to use. Errors are easily rectified and slight irregularities do not detract from the final effect. A gilded surface is not the most robust of finishes, so be gentle when planting up.

1 *Ensure the pot is free from dust and grease and is completely dry. Seal terracotta and porous surfaces with PVA and allow to dry. Use a wide paintbrush to apply a thin, even coat of size to all the surfaces to be gilded. Leave it to dry for about 25 minutes.*

LEFT A simple trough is made splendid by a layer of imitation silver leaf, which gives it chic sophistication. Gold or copper leaf creates a totally different effect, so don't be afraid to experiment.

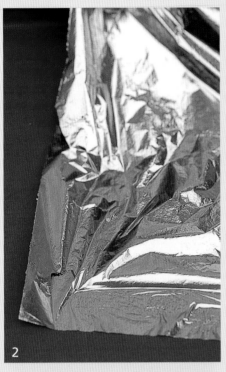

2 Gently take a sheet of metal and lay it on the surface of the pot – it will stick as soon as it touches the size. Repeat this process, allowing the sheets to overlap slightly, until the whole surface is covered.

3 The metal sheets are very light and seem difficult to handle but remember that tears can be repaired, creases smoothed out and gaps filled by adding small pieces of leaf and smoothing them into place.

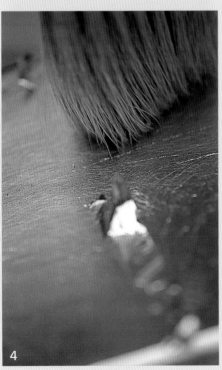

4 Next smooth the sheets down using a soft cloth or paintbrush, removing any excess metal leaf where the sheets overlap, and smoothing out tears and creases. Allow the container to dry for 24 hours.

5 Using a dust-free paintbrush, give the whole container a coat of clear exterior varnish to protect the surface. Once the varnish is dry the container is ready to plant.

marbling

There is a plethora of marbles and marbling effects, some of which are easier to create than others. This is a veined marble, perhaps best described as a fantasy marble, which is easy to create with just a few basic tools.

A marbled finish can be created in any combination of colours to suit any planting scheme or location. You could stick to a natural palate, aiming to imitate real stone, or go wild and create something unique and daring.

You will need three colours: here a cream base is decorated with yellow and red artists' acrylics, which mix together in the marbling process to give clouds of orange and yellow with striking red veins. The acrylics are mixed with a little scumble glaze, available from craft shops, to stop them drying too quickly, allowing time to perfect the finish.

It is a good idea to practise your planned marble on a piece of board or paper first, although if things do go wrong on the container you can always apply another base coat and start again. If you would like a glossy finish, a coat of outdoor polyurethane can be applied once the marbling is dry, but this is not essential.

RIGHT This fantasy marble uses bright colours to create a really eye-catching container, but you could use natural shades to imitate real marble. When marbling, keep assessing what you have done and don't overdo it – it is often better to stop before you think you have finished. You can always add a little more detail later.

1

1 *Prepare the container with an appropriate sealant (see page 128). Apply a light base coat of acrylic paint – white or cream, or a very pale shade of the final colour.*

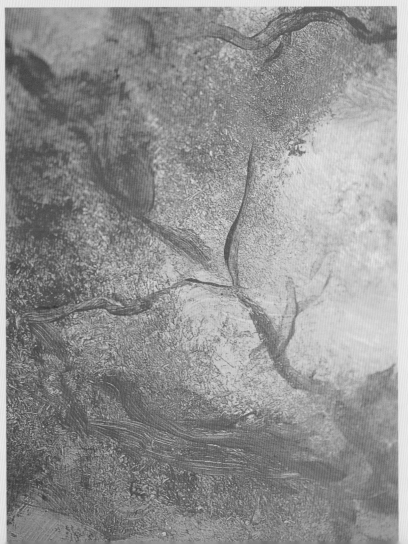

2 *When the base coat is dry, dilute some of the light acrylic paint with a little scumble. Use a large brush to roll the paint onto the pot in an irregular diagonal, like the veining of real marble. Next use a small stippling brush to work over the paint, stamping it up and down and blurring the edges a little.*

3 *Large pots and containers can be worked in sections if necessary. While the first colour is still wet, dilute some of the darker acrylic paint, in this case red, with a little scumble and apply it in the same diagonal rolling strokes.*

4 *Stipple the darker colour in the same way as the lighter one, stamping the small brush up and down to blur the edges of the strokes. This time, allow the two colours to mix as you stipple.*

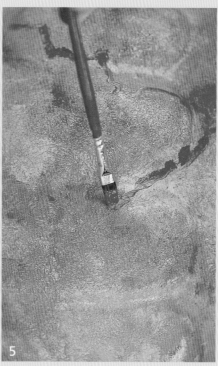

5 *Finally, add some veining. Use a small artists' brush and roll the paint onto the pot in a loose, irregular line in the same fashion as before. Some veins might branch or fade out. Keep taking time to stand back and assess the effect before adding more. Often it is best to stop before you think you should.*

mosaic

Whether it is composed of glass mosaic tesserae, broken china or ceramic tiles, mosaic offers an inspiring and durable finish.

The method used to apply a mosaic finish is straightforward and the same whatever material you are using and whatever the design you create.

Outdoor tile cements and grouts are used to achieve a finish that will really stand up to the elements. Terracotta, concrete and stone provide a good firm foundation for a mosaic surface and are easy to work on. Metal and plastic pose a few more problems as the container is likely to move or expand and contract with changes in temperature, causing the mosaic surface to loosen and ultimately fall off. This problem is overcome by adding a compound to the tile cement to make it highly flexible.

1 *First clean and seal the container (see page 128). If you are using sheets of mosaic tesserae, cut pieces to fit the sides of the container. Mix up a quantity of tile cement according to the manufacturer's instructions and apply a thin, even bed of cement to the container in a manageable area.*

2 *Next gently position the mosaic tiles on the container and push them into place. If you are using individual tiles or pieces of broken china, push the pieces into the cement, leaving an even gap between them. Continue until the whole container is covered.*

3 *When the cement is dry, mix up the grout according to the manufacturer's instructions. Use a spatula, sponge or squeegee to spread the grout over the surface of the mosaic, forcing it into the spaces between the tiles. Remove the excess from the surface.*

4 *When the grout has been allowed to dry a little, polish off any final traces of it from the surface of the tiles using a soft cloth. Allow to dry thoroughly then plant up the container.*

pewtering

A striking finish for garden containers, a pewter effect lends instant weight, solidity and grandeur to any container, even plastic ones, although on plainer pots its appeal can be quite contemporary.

The pewter effect is deceptively easy to achieve and can be reasonably hard wearing. Any wear and tear is easily patched up or passed off as shabby chic. The finish can be applied to any surface with the correct preparation (see page 128) and takes little time to create. You can make your container as silvery or dark as you wish, but stand back and assess your progress every now and again.

1 *Apply a coat of the correct primer to a clean dry container. Allow to dry thoroughly.*

2 *Next give the entire container a coat of dark grey paint. Allow the paint to dry completely, then add a second coat, aiming for a smooth, even coverage. Allow to dry again.*

3 *Apply silver gilding cream to the raised areas of the pot to create highlights. Work the gilding cream out from these areas and fade the silvery finish into the grey paint.*

plant care

To give plants the best possible start, it pays to go back to basics and ensure they are planted correctly in the right compost and provided with the best growing conditions possible. To keep container displays looking good, they will need watering and feeding as well as an occasional tidy up.

planting

For best results, containers should have drainage holes in the bottom to let excess moisture drain away, and should be big enough to contain enough compost for the plants. If you are concerned about stability, place a brick or concrete block in the base to add weight, if space allows.

1 To ensure good drainage, put a layer of crocks, pieces of broken terracotta pot or pebbles in the base of the container. Pieces of polystyrene make a lightweight alternative for wall pots or containers used on roofs or balconies.

2 Half-fill the container with compost and, with the plants still in their pots, arrange them in the trough, planning the display. Remember to consider the ultimate heights and habits of the plants.

3 When you are happy with the arrangement, carefully remove a plant from its pot by spreading your hand over the top of the pot and inverting it – the plant should land neatly in your hand. Place the plant in the trough. Repeat this process with all the plants.

4 Now add compost around the plants, being careful not to leave any air spaces and tucking the compost firmly around the rootballs. The level of the compost should be about 5 cm (2 in) from the top of the container and the plants should be planted to the same depth as they were in their pots.

5 Next water the plants in well, taking care to water the compost and avoid foliage and flowers. If you are using a mulch, spread it on the surface once you have watered.

composts

To ensure your container plants are in top health, vigorous and flower abundantly, it is important to provide the right growing medium or compost – there are three basic choices.

Never be tempted to use soil from your garden – it is likely to harbour pests, diseases and weed seeds and the nutritional content may be inappropriate. Some gardeners mix their own composts but for most of us it is much better to buy a suitable compost. There are two main types: loam based and peat based. Loam-based composts contain good-quality sterilized loam, while peat-based composts contain mainly peat or peat substitute. They have different characteristics and are suited to different types of container planting.

Loam-based composts

Where plants will spend several seasons in their containers, a loam-based compost is perfect as it has a high organic content and plenty of nutrition to sustain growth over a long period of time. In addition, its structure means that it is less likely to become waterlogged and airless, and it also loses moisture more slowly than peat-based compost. It is usually sold in different grades, depending on the level of nutrition in the compost, so choose a compost recommended for the plants you are using.

Peat-based composts

Peat-based potting composts are used a great deal in container gardening and are best suited to short-term displays of annuals, or perhaps perennials that are intended for the garden at the end of the season. These composts have the advantage of being inexpensive and light. However, peat extraction has unfortunate environmental consequences and for that reason there are peat-free container composts based on alternatives such as coir. Peat-based composts have several drawbacks: they tend to become easily waterlogged if the container is overwatered, yet dry out easily if underwatered. This type of compost contains only enough nutrients for a few weeks of growth, so use a liquid feed to keep plants growing healthily or, alternatively, a slow-release fertilizer can be mixed with the compost before planting (see page 141).

Ericaceous compost

Acid-loving plants, such as rhododendrons, azaleas and some heathers, require ericaceous compost. This is a loam-based compost with a low pH, which will create the acidic conditions these plants need to thrive.

ABOVE Loam-based compost is a dark grey and feels heavy.

LEFT Peat-based compost is light in texture and brown in colour.

mulches

A mulch is a layer of material spread over the surface of the compost. Mulches can take many different forms and their benefits are both practical and aesthetic.

Mulch will reduce the evaporation of water from compost and even-out changes in soil temperature. Applying a mulch also has the advantage of suppressing the growth of weeds.

A carefully selected mulch can add to the impact of a container, acting as the visual link between plant and pot. In some situations the dark brown of the compost works well, in others it is inevitable that there will be no compost visible as the plants thrive and spill over the edges of the container. Sometimes, however, there is a definite gap to be filled between plant and pot. Practical and inexpensive, a layer of grit creates a neat, inconspicuous finish to the tops of pots. Choosing one of the many coloured gravels or glass mulches available can give the opportunity to reinforce a colour theme or provide the perfect foil for foliage and flowers.

Lime-green foliage emerging from sparking blue glass mulch will have much more impact than the same foliage emerging from compost, while the black strap-like leaves of *Ophiopogon planiscapus* 'Nigrescens' are lost on the surface of compost but sing out on a mulch of cream gravel.

All sorts of materials can be pressed into service as a mulch – fir cones, nuts, buttons, beads or shells all work well in the right situation and add some fine detail to the display.

TOP LEFT TO BOTTOM RIGHT Grey and cream cobbles, crushed black glass mulch, crushed blue glass mulch, crushed shell mulch, blue cobbles, and blue slate.

daily care

While some plants seem to thrive on neglect, most need a little regular care and attention in the form of feeding and watering to look their best. And a general tidy-up from time to time works wonders.

Watering

Plants in containers have only a very small reserve of moisture to draw on. In warm weather they are completely dependant on the water you provide and even in showery weather they may need watering if the rainfall is not sufficient or if they are in a sheltered location or the foliage prevents the rain from reaching the compost. Obviously smaller containers are more prone to drying out than larger ones.

The best way to judge if a plant needs watering is to feel the compost below the surface. If the compost feels moist, do not water. Overwatering can be just as damaging as under-watering. There should be plenty of warning signs, allowing time for the situation to be rectified before plants die of either under- or overwatering. Often the most wilted plant can be revived with a good soaking.

Peat-based composts can be hard to rehydrate once they have dried out. The simplest solution is to submerge the whole pot in a bucket of water and leave it until the water permeates all the way through the compost. Tap water is fine for watering most plants, the exception being acid-loving plants. For these plants, use rainwater.

If you are watering with a watering can, always water the compost only, avoiding leaves and flowers. A gentle flow ensures that the compost is not disturbed. Labour-saving, automatic irrigation systems are widely available – once set up, the drip heads supply water to individual containers. There are some drawbacks to these systems, however. They can be unsightly and difficult to hide and the location of the containers is limited by the extent of the system.

Feeding

Loam-based composts contain enough fertilizer to sustain plants for several growing seasons; peat-based composts are relatively poor in nutrition so extra feeding will be needed to ensure a really good display of healthy plants at their best. A simple option is to incorporate a slow-release fertilizer with the potting compost before you plant up the container. Releasing nutrition into the soil over a period of months, these products should provide a steady supply of food over the growing period. The alternative is a liquid feed that needs to be applied either to the compost or the foliage of the plants at regular intervals in accordance with the manufacturer's instructions. Fast acting, these feeds are perfect for quickly perking up plants that are failing to perform.

Tidying and deadheading

Keeping containers looking good is an easy job and can be incredibly satisfying. The main task for displays of annuals is to remove faded blooms. This not only stops the display looking tatty, but encourages a plant to produce new flowers. Dead flowerheads are easily pinched or snipped off. In a mixed container, dominant plants need to be kept in check to prevent them swamping their less rampant fellows. To encourage other plants to adopt a bushy habit and fill out, pinch out their growing tips as they grow.

Permanently planted containers will need tidying in autumn and spring. Herbaceous perennials and grasses can be left standing through the winter, their dead foliage and seedheads providing an arresting display sparkling with frost. In early spring the dead foliage can be cut back to make way for the new season's growth.

LEFT Remove dead flowers as they fade to encourage the plant to produce more blooms, rather than making seed.

INDEX

AUTHOR'S ACKNOWLEDGEMENTS

My thanks to:

Tim Sharples of Cedar Nurseries, Cobham, Surrey and David Manetti of Europa Impruneta for giving us the opportunity to shoot their magnificent Impruneta terracotta.

The staff of Grovelands Garden Centre, Shinfield, Reading, especially Darren Corbett, for all their help and always having just the right plant.

Jean Harper for enthusiastically producing the colourful marble paint effects of my imaginings.

The Netherlands Flower Bulb Information Centre for supplying a fantastic array of bulbs that performed beautifully, producing fantastic blooms and vibrant colour.

My parents, Ruth and Geoffrey Smee, once again, for their willingness to help with anything and everything.

And finally to Clive Nichols and Joanna Smith who have worked so hard on this project from the very beginning, not only contributing their special skills – Clive his superlative photography and Jo her editing and design prowess – but also their enthusiasm and much valued friendship.

CREDITS

Executive Editor Sarah Ford
Executive Art Director Peter Burt
Editor and Designer Joanna Smith
Production Controller Ian Paton

**All photographs © Clive Nichols
All projects and photographs designed and styled by Clare Matthews, except the following:**
p7 Lisette Pleasance; p12 & p20 right Keukenhof Gardens, Holland; p22 left Philip Blake; p23 left Andy Sturgeon Circ Garden, Chelsea 2001; p24 top left Keukenhof Gardens, Holland; p24 bottom left Robin Green and Ralph Cade; p26 top Hedens Lustgard, Sweden; p26 bottom Stephen Woodhams; p28 left Jenny Jowett; p28 bottom right The Nichols Garden, Reading, lighting by Garden & Security Lighting; p29 top right Keukenhof Gardens, Holland; p29 left Robin Green and Ralph Cade; p31 top Nyewood House, West Sussex; p31 bottom Jane Rendell/Sarah Tavender, Hampton Court 2001; p120 right, p121 & p123 Europa Impruneta, Tuscany, Italy.